Robert Burns
for Beginners

Robert Burns
for
Beginners

RENNIE McOWAN

Rowan Tree Publishing

First published in 1995, and reprinted in 1996, 1998, 2001

This edition published in 2014 by
ROWAN TREE PUBLISHING
Lochbank House, Castle Douglas DG7 1TH

ISBN 978-0-9562307-7-5

British Library Cataloguing in Publication Data
A catalogue record for this book is available from the British Library.

Editorial consultant: Patricia Burgess
Cover and design: Annette Peppis & Associates
Cover photograph: Leo Blamire
Violin by courtesy of the estate of Mr Thomas Mooney

Picture credits: p51 Ḥulinska Yevheniia/Shutterstock; p69 serazetdinov/ Shutterstock

Printed and bound in Scotland

ACKNOWLEDGEMENTS

Special thanks are due to Susan Smelt of Milton of Campsie, who in April 1994 won a National Certificate of Merit for Excellence in project work on Robert Burns presented by the Burns Federation, and who made helpful suggestions towards this book.

Thanks are also due to Jimmy Black for his wise advice and encouragement; and to A.G. Barr plc for their permission to use the product Irn-Bru® on the cover of this book.

NOTES FOR READERS

The format of this book has been designed in such a way as to help readers grasp the main aspects of a Burns Supper. The aim is that they should understand the background that has led to the present-day form of a Burns Supper, and be encouraged to organise one for themselves at home or in school.

Questions, Things to Do and Follow-up Exercises are features of this book. They offer younger readers the opportunity to think about what they have read, and then to work on individual or shared projects. While they can go online to help them with their fact-finding searches, they could also visit a public library and consult the reference books listed on page 87.

CONTENTS

e first is Gaelic, a language
ago. Today it is spoken m
s. Robert Burns could no
ortant language and he

Happy Birthday Robert Burns

January 25th is a very special day. Why? Because one of the world's best-known poets was born on that day in 1759. This poet was born in Alloway, a little village in Ayrshire, Scotland. What was the name of this poet? His name was Robert Burns.

Every year, in the month of January, people in many different countries remember Robert Burns. Why is that? Because the poems and songs of this man from Alloway are so popular that they have been translated into many languages. For example, one of his songs – 'Auld Lang Syne' – is sung all over the world when people want to remember being happy together. They sing it just before they have to say goodbye and leave each other.

Lines and verses from poems by Robert Burns are admired and remembered by people all over the world. They are often repeated by other writers – in books, plays, scripts for radio and television, and so on. These repetitions are called 'quotations', and these quotations are often used by famous men and women when making public speeches.

People use these quotations because Robert's verses are so clever and well written. They use them because the words mean a lot to them. The words can make them happy or sad. Perhaps they want to say something important or funny or special – and they cannot find quite the right words to say it for themselves – and, anyway, they know that Robert Burns said it better than they ever could.

So they think he's brilliant! They really enjoy the poems and sometimes learn them off by heart. Yes, they remember Robert Burns and they honour him.

What are Robert's poems like? Well, some are long. Some are short. Some are in the English language. Some are in Scots. Some are in both. When reading his poems you will know most of the words he uses, but if you don't, you can always ask someone – such as your teacher, your mother or father, a friend or someone at your local library.

We are very lucky in Scotland because we have three beautiful languages.

The first is Gaelic, a language spoken in many parts of Scotland long ago. Today it is spoken mainly in parts of the Highlands and Islands. Robert Burns could not speak Gaelic, but he knew it was an important language and he respected it.

The second language is Scots, which is a dialect or variation of English. It is not spoken all the time these days, but most Scottish people know lots of Scots words. They are very rich words. They are strong words. They are colourful words. People in country areas, towns and villages still use Scots words. We should be proud of these words. They are part of our Scottish heritage. It is good to know these words.

You might have friends who live in another city, town or village. Have you ever noticed that some of the words they say sound different from the way that you say them? And they will think that you sound different from them. These differences are called 'accents'. For example, the word 'fish' is pronounced 'fush' or 'feesh' in different parts of the country. Or – another example – the word 'no' is pronounced 'nae' (nay) or sometimes 'na'. Can you think of any other words like this?

Sometimes, in different parts of Scotland, we use a different word to mean the same thing – for example, the words 'chiel' and 'loon' both mean a 'lad' or 'fellow', and 'quean' and 'lass' mean a 'young woman'. These words are part of our local dialect.

Another example – a 'forkie-tail' and a 'clipshear' are the same thing. Find out what this is by looking up a dictionary of the Scots language. In which areas of Scotland are these words used?

Lots of these words, even those still used today, were once part of the old Scots language. It is good that they are still used in some form or other. They are, after all, part of our heritage in Scotland. Try to use them if you can.

Robert Burns certainly loved Scots words and the Scots language. His poetry is full of Scots words.

The third language used in Scotland is modern English. Robert Burns wrote in that language as well. Today nearly all of us speak in modern English. Television uses modern English. It too is a beautiful language.

So remember – Robert Burns liked Gaelic. He liked English. But most of all he liked the Scots language. It was the language of the people of his time and it is still around in many ways in the language we speak and use today in Scotland.

◦ ◦ ◦

groaning trencher there ye
r pin wad help to mend a n
s the dews distil Like amb
ht. An cut you up wi rea

Who is Robert Burns?

Your hurdies like a distant
...time o' need, While thro...
...d. His knife see Rustic-lab...
...ght, Trenching your gushi...

Robert Burns' mother and father were not rich people. They had a small house in Alloway, Ayrshire, which Robert's father, William, built himself. William (1721–84) worked as gardener to the local provost. Before this, William Burns (or 'Burnes', as the surname was often spelt) was recorded as a tenant farmer of Alloway when he married Agnes Broun (1732–1820) of Craigenton, Maybole.

Their son Robert was born on 25 January 1759. In 1766, while the poet-to-be was still a young boy, William rented a farm at Mount Oliphant, near Alloway. This can still be seen today.

Robert did not go to school as children do today. His father and other farmers in the area paid money to hire a teacher for their children. Robert liked reading best. This helped him to become a great poet later on.

Robert and his brothers worked very hard on their parents' farm, even as small children. In fact, some people think Robert worked a bit too hard on the farm. He was often out in the cold and rain and the work was back-breaking. This may be part of the reason why he became ill with angina and rheumatic fever in later life.

The Burns family moved again in 1777 – this time to a farm called Lochlea (sometimes spelt 'Lochlie') in Tarbolton, also in Ayrshire. Sadly, the family found farm life very difficult there.

But things were not all bad. When Robert was in his twenties, he and his friends formed a club where they could meet together socially from time to time. They met in Tarbolton and spent the evenings arguing with one another, learning to dance and talking about girls. The club, called the Tarbolton Bachelors' Club, was for men and boys only. (A 'bachelor' is an unmarried man.) Do you think a club just for men and boys is fair? It was the fashion then. Women and girls were not allowed to become members.

If you visit Tarbolton, you can still see the building where the club was held.

As Robert grew up, he began to write poems for girls he liked. But he began to write other poems as well. And sometimes he wrote words to match tunes that people already knew.

Robert was only 25 years old when his father died. The family moved to another farm after that. It was called Mossgiel and was near Mauchline in Ayrshire.

By this time Robert was a popular man with the ladies and he had lots of girlfriends. Some people thought he was too fond of attending parties, drinking and having a good time. They felt he should start behaving in a more responsible way.

When some church people criticised him, Robert became angry with the Church itself. He thought these people were being too narrow-minded. So he criticised them back, sometimes in his poems. 'Holy Willie's Prayer' is a good example of this.

In 1786 a book of poems by Robert Burns was published. People read it and told others to read it, and soon lots of men and women were reading it. He became famous – everyone was reading the poems of Robert Burns!

So off Robert went to Scotland's capital city, Edinburgh, where important people went out of their way to meet him – publishers, printers, lawyers and titled people, such as the Marquis of Graham, the Duke of Portland and the Duke of Montague.

Robert also took time to visit other parts of Scotland, including the Highlands. He loved the beautiful sweeping landscapes there.

A second book of poems was published on 31 July 1786. Like the previous volume, the new book became very popular. Robert was now becoming as well known to everyone then as a film star or pop singer or famous footballer is today.

Just like these modern versions of himself, Robert didn't always behave very well, especially with girlfriends. He often managed to get himself into a lot of trouble with their parents and friends. However, Robert could also be extremely sensitive and gentle. He could be thoughtful too. Some of the beautiful love songs and poems he wrote are now famous all over the world.

Burns eventually married a girl called Jean Armour and they had a large family together. He rented a farm called Ellisland, near Dumfries, and built a home there for his wife and children.

As time went on, Robert needed more money because a family can cost a lot to keep in food and clothes. So he found himself another job. He became an exciseman, like a modern-day customs officer. His job was to stop people smuggling goods and trying to make whisky in secret to avoid paying a government tax called 'duty'. Because of the type of work an exciseman had to do, it was not a popular job. Robert wrote a poem and song about it called 'The Deil's awa with Exciseman'. It tells how the Devil had taken the exciseman away – and lots of people were very glad about that.

At the same time Robert kept working on his farm. It was a hard life. No wonder he became very ill and had to give up the farm.

Robert had to work very hard at his job as an exciseman. He had to travel a lot on horseback and it was very tiring. His health really suffered. So doctors sent him to the Solway Firth to sea-bathe – they thought it would help to cure his illness. We know nowadays that this was not a wise thing to do – in fact, it only made matters worse.

Robert and his wife Jean had more children – in fact, nine in total – but sadly Robert was not destined to live much longer. He died on 21 July 1796. He was only 37 years old.

However, the poems and songs of Robert Burns live on. Let us now look at some of them.

ee sleekit, cow'rin, tim'rou
stie! Thou need na start a
d be laith to run an chase t
rry man's dominion Has

Robert Burns and the Mouse

*stie, O, what a panic's in t
e hasty; Wi bickering bratt
Wi murdering pattle! I'm
n Nature's social union*

More and more books of Robert's poems were published after his death, until he became well known all over the world. Robert wrote all kinds of poems. He wrote sad poems and joyful poems. He loved the countryside and wrote about small things, such as mice and daisies. He wanted everyone to enjoy a good life and not to be hungry or poor or feel threatened. Instead they should have dignity and freedom. He loved Scotland and praised the country in his poems and songs. These were the subjects that interested him.

On the next page you will find a famous Burns short poem called 'To a Mouse'. This is how it came to be written. One day, when Robert was out in the fields ploughing, the blade (known as a 'coulter') cut into the nest of a mouse. Robert was very sorry to have disturbed or hurt the mouse inside, and this is a poem about his feelings. (Any puzzling words are explained at the end of the poem.)

◦ ◦ ◦

To a Mouse

ON TURNING HER UP IN HER NEST WITH THE PLOUGH
~ NOVEMBER 1785 ~

Wee sleekit, cow'rin, tim'rous beastie,
O, what a panic's in thy breastie!
Thou need na start awa sae hasty;
    Wi bickering brattle!
I wad be laith to run an chase thee,
    Wi murdering pattle!

I'm truly sorry man's dominion
Has broken Nature's social union,
An justifies that ill opinion,
    Which makes thee startle
At me, thy poor, earth-born companion,
    An fellow mortal!

I doubt na, whyles, but thou may thieve;
What then? poor beastie, thou maun live!
A daimen icker in a thrave
    'S a sma request;
I'll get a blessin wi the lave,
    An never miss't!

Thy wee-bit housie, too, in ruin!
Its silly wa's the win's are strewin!
An naething, now, to big a new ane,
    O foggage green!
An bleak December's win's ensuin,
Baith snell an keen!

Thou saw the fields laid bare an waste,
An weary winter comin fast,
An cozie here, beneath the blast,
     Thou thought to dwell,
Till crash! The cruel coulter past
     Out thro' thy cell.

That wee bit heap o' leaves an stibble,
Has cost thee monie a weary nibble!
Now thou's turn'd out, for a' thy trouble,
     But house or hald,
To thole the winter's sleety dribble,
     An cranreuch cauld!

But Mousie, thou art no thy lane,
In proving foresight may be vain:
The best-laid schemes o' mice an men
     Gang aft agley,
An lea'e us nought but grief an pain,
     For promis'd joy!

Still thou art blest, compar'd wi me!
The present only toucheth thee:
But och! I backward case my e'e,
     On prospects drear!
An forward, tho I canna see
     I guess an fear!

WORD LIST

bickering brattle	=	a hurrying scamper
coulter	=	a plough-blade
cranreuch cauld	=	hoar frost
daimen icker in a thrave	=	an extra ear in 24 sheaves of corn or barley
foggage green	=	coarse grass
gang aft agley	=	often go wrong
laith	=	loth, reluctant, sorry to …
lave	=	the rest, the remainder
maun	=	must
pattle	=	a plough-scraper
sleekit	=	smooth or glossy-coated
snell	=	bitter, severe
thole	=	to endure
whyles	=	at times

QUESTIONS

- Robert Burns didn't mean to hurt the little mouse.
  Why then do you think he was so upset?
- He calls the mouse a 'fellow mortal'. What does he mean?
- What does he mean by saying:
  'A daimen icker in a thrave / 'S a sma request'?
- Is he angry that the mouse has been eating his corn or barley?

○ ○ ○

- The poet says:
  'The best-laid schemes o' mice an men / Gang aft agley.'
  What feeling is he sharing with the mouse?

○ ○ ○

- Do you think 'To a Mouse' is an important poem?
- Is the poet just feeling sorry that he has wrecked the mouse's home, or is he telling us something else too? What else might he be trying to say?
- Robert Burns wrote this poem in November 1785. Why do you think it is still a popular poem today?

THINGS TO DO

- Why not draw a picture of Robert Burns ploughing?
  You could draw him, the plough and the mouse.
  You might draw the mouse looking up at him, and the coulter (blade) of the plough just before the mouse runs away.
- Do you know what a furrow is?
  Try drawing some furrows in a field.
- Why not make a model of Burns, the plough and the mouse?

FOLLOW-UP EXERCISE

◎ Robert Burns wrote another poem that resembled 'To a Mouse'
when he cut down a daisy with his plough. It is called 'To a
Mountain Daisy'. He wrote this poem of nine verses in April
1786. Here is the first verse:

> Wee, modest, crimson-tippèd flow'r,
> Thou's met me in an evil hour;
> For I maun crush among the stoure
> > Thy slender stem:
> To spare thee now is past my pow'r,
> > Thou bonie gem.

◎ Do you think Robert was sorry to destroy the daisy, even though
it was an accident?

◎ Do you know what 'maun' means?

◎ Do you know what 'stoure' means?

◎ You might like to draw Robert Burns' plough cutting down the
daisy, or make a model of this incident.

arlocks and witches in a da
nce, But hornpipes, jigs, s
le in their heels, A winnoc
ick, in shape o' beast; A t

Tam O' Shanter's Big Adventure

A re you afraid of witches? There was a man called Tam O'
Shanter who certainly was! He was out riding on his horse –
a mare called Maggie (Meg for short) – when he saw a lot of
witches. It happened at a church called Alloway Kirk in Ayrshire, a
place that local people thought was haunted.

Tam only escaped because his horse could gallop very fast when
she had to and because – as the story tells us – witches cannot cross
running water, such as the burn in this story.

But even though Meg was fast, one of the witches got very, very
close and grabbed at the poor horse's tail, pulling most of the hair
out. Some waterfalls are called the 'Grey Mare's Tail' after this part
of the story because falling water looks a bit like a horse's tail.
Perhaps there is a Grey Mare's Tail waterfall near you?

Robert wrote about this local story in a poem that he called
'Tam O' Shanter'. This poem is quite frightening in places, but parts
of it are very funny as well, and it makes many people laugh. It is
called an 'epic' poem, meaning that it is very long and has a hero
in it – Tam!

'Tam O' Shanter' is also a very famous poem and it is recited
each year at special events called Burns Suppers. (You will find out
about these suppers on pages 53–85.) Some people learn the poem
by heart. This is not easy because, as we have said, it is a long poem
– a *very* long poem – but it always gets lots of applause and cheers
when it is recited.

○ ○ ○

The Story of the Poem

Tam has been to market, but it is now late at night and he must think about going home. This is not as easy as it may seem, however, because Tam has drunk too much beer and whisky. His wife, Kate, always gets very angry with him for getting drunk, and Tam knows that he'll be in a lot of trouble when he gets home.

Astride his grey mare Maggie, slowly plodding along the path, Tam approaches the church of Alloway Kirk. There he is amazed – no, *shocked!* – to see a crowd of witches and warlocks dancing in the kirk-yard. (A 'warlock' is a male witch.) Even the Devil himself is there, playing the bagpipes!

One young witch is dancing so well that she catches Tam's eye. He roars with delight – 'Weel done, Cutty-sark'. ('Cutty-sark' means 'short shirt' or 'chemise', which is what the dancer was wearing.)

Suddenly there is silence. The witches stop their dancing … they spot the slightly tipsy Tam and begin to chase him.

Tam spurs his horse and gallops away for his life, escaping … but only just.

This is a great poem, full of lovely images. Enjoy it!

Tam O' Shanter
A Tale

OF BROWNYIS AND OF BOGILLIS FULL IS THIS BUKE.
~ GAWIN DOUGLAS ~

When chapman billies leave the street,
And drouthy neebors, neebors meet;
As market-days are wearing late,
An folk begin to tak the gate;
While we sit bousing at the nappy,
An getting fou and unco happy,
We think na on the lang Scots miles,
The mosses, waters, slaps, and styles,
That lie between us and our hame,
Where sits our sulky, sullen dame,
Gathering her bows like gathering storm,
Nursing her wrath to keep it warm.

This truth fand honest Tam O' Shanter,
As he frae Ayr ae night did canter:
(Auld Ayr, whom ne'er a town surpasses,
For honest men and bonie lasses).

O Tam hadst thou but been sae wise,
As taen thy ain wife Kate's advice!
She tauld thee well thou was a skellum,
A blethering, blustering, drunken blellum;
That frae November will October,
Ae market-day thou was nae sober;
That ilka melder wi the miller,
Thou sat as lang as thou had siller;

That ev'ry naig was ca'd a shoe on,
The smith and thee gat roarin fou on;
That at the Lord's house, even on Sunday,
Thou drank wi Kirkton Jean till Monday.
She prophesied that, late or soon,
Thou would be found, deep drown'd in Doon,
Or catch'd wi warlocks in the mirk,
By Alloway's auld, haunted kirk.

Ah, gentle dames, it gives me greet,
To think how monie counsels sweet,
How monie lengthen'd, sage advices
The husband frae the wife despises!

But to our tale: – Ae market-night,
Tam had got planted unco right,
Fast by an ingle, bleezing finely,
Wi reaming swats, that drank divinely;
And at his elbow, Souter Johnie,
His ancient, trusty, drouthy cronie:
Tam lo'ed him like a very brither;
They had been fou for weeks thegither,
The night drave on wi sangs and clatter;
And ay the ale was growing better:
The landlady and Tam grew gracious,
Wi secret favours, sweet and precious:
The Souter tauld his queerest stories;
The landlord's laugh was ready chorus:
The storm without might rair and rustle,
Tam did na mind the storm a whistle.

Care, mad to see man sae happy,
E'en drown'd himself amang the nappy.
As bees flee hame wi lades o' treasure,
The minutes wing'd their way wi pleasure:
Kings may be blest but Tam was glorious,
O'er a' the ills o' life victorious!

But pleasures are like poppies spread:
You seize the flow'r, its bloom is shed;
Or like the snow falls in the river,
A moment white – then melts for ever;
Or like the borealis race,
That flit ere you can point their place;
Or like the rainbow's lovely form
Evanishing amid the storm.
Nae man can tether time or tide,
The hour approaches Tam maun ride:
That hour o' night's black arch the key-stane,
That dreary hour Tam mounts his beast in:
And sic a night he taks the road in,
As ne'er poor sinner was abroad in.

The wind blew as 'twad blawn its last;
The rattling showers rose on the blast;
The speedy gleams the darkness swallow'd;
Loud, deep, and lang the thunder bellow'd;
That night, a child might understand,
The Deil had business on his hand.

Weel mounted on his grey mare Meg,
A better never lifted leg,

Tam skelpit on thro dub and mire,
Despising wind, and rain, and fire;
Whiles holding fast his guid blue bonnet,
Whiles crooning o'er some auld Scots sonnet,
Whiles glow'ring round wi prudent cares,
Lest bogles catch him unawares:
Alloway Kirk was drawing nigh,
Whare ghaists and houlets nightly cry.

By this time he was cross the ford,
Whare in the snaw the chapman smoor'd;
And past the birks and meikle stane,
Where drunken Charlie brak's neck-bane;
And thro the whins, and by the cairn,
Where hunters fand the murder'd bairn;
And near the thorn, aboon the well,
Where Mungo's mither hang'd hersel.
Before him Doon pours all his floods;
The doubling storm roars thro the woods;
The lightnings flash from pole to pole,
Near and more near the thunders roll:
When, glimmering thro the groaning trees,
Alloway Kirk seem'd in a bleeze,
Thro ilka bore the beams were glancing,
And loud resounded mirth and dancing.

Inspiring bold John Barleycorn,
What dangers thou canst make us scorn!
Wi tippenny, we fear nae evil;
Wi usquabae, we'll face the Devil!
The swats sae ream'd in Tammie's noddle,

Fair play, he car'd na deils a boddle.
But Maggie stood, right sair astonish'd,
Till, by the heel and hand admonish'd,
She ventur'd forward on the light;
And, wow! Tam saw an unco sight!

Warlocks and witches in a dance:
Nae cotillion, brent new frae France,
But hornpipes, jigs, strathspeys, and reels,
Put life and mettle in their heels,
A winnock-bunker in the east,
There sat Auld Nick, in shape o' beast;
A tousie tyke, black, grim and large,
To gie them music was his charge:
He screw'd the pipes and gart them skirl,
Till roof and rafters a' did dirl.
Coffins stood round, like open presses,
That shaw'd the dead in their last dresses;
And, by some devilish cantraip sleight,
Each in its cauld hand held a light:
By which heroic Tam was able
To note upon the holy table,
A murderer's banes, in gibbet-airns;
Twa span-lang, wee, unchristen'd bairns;
A thief new-cutted frae a rape –
Wi his last gasp his gab die gape;
Five tomahawks, wi blude red-rusted.
Five scymitars, wi murder crusted;
A garter which a babe had strangled,
A knife a father's throat had mangled –

Whom his ain son o' life bereft –
The grey-hairs yet stack to the heft;
Wi mair of horrible and awefu,
Which even to name wad be unlawfu.
Three Lawyers' tongues, turned inside out,
Wi' lies seamed like a beggar's clout;
Three Priests' hearts rotten, black as muck,
Lay stinking, vile, in every neuk.

As Tammie glowr'd, amaz'd and curious,
The mirth and fun grew fast and furious;
The piper loud and louder blew,
The dancers quick and quicker flew,
They reel'd, they set, they cross'd, they cleekit,
Till ilka carlin swat and reekit,
And coost her duddies to the wark,
And linket at it in her sark!

Now Tam, o' Tam! had thae been queans,
A plump and strapping in their teens!
Their sarks, instead o' creeshie flannen,
Been snaw-white seventeen hunder linen! –
Thir breeks o' mine, my only pair,
That ance were plush, o' guid blue hair,
I wad hae gien them off my hurdies,
For ae blink o' the bonie burdies!
But wither'd beldams, auld and droll,
Rigwoodie hags and spean a foal,
Louping and flinging on a crummock,
I wonder did na turn thy stomach!

But Tam kend what was what fu brawlie:
There was ae winsome wench and wawlie,

That night enlisted in the core,
Lang after kend on Carrick shore
(For monie a beast to dead she shot,
An perish'd monie a bonie boat,
And shook baith meikle corn and bear,
And kept the country-side in fear).
Her cutty sark, o' Paisley harn,
That while a lassie she had worn,
In longitude tho sorely scanty,
It was her best, and she was vauntie …
Ah! little kend thy reverend grannie,
That sark she coft for her wee Nannie,
Wi twa pund Scots ('twas a' her riches),
Wad ever grac'd a dance of witches!

But here my Muse her wing maun cour,
Six flights are far beyond her power:
To sing how Nannie lap and flang
(A souple jade she was and strang),
And how Tam stood like ane bewitch'd,
And thought his very een enrich'd;
Even Satan glowr'd, and fidg'd fu fain,
And hotch'd and blew wi might and main:
Till first ae caper, syne anither,
Tam tint his reason a' thegither,
And roars out, 'Weel done, Cutty-sark!'
And in an instant all was dark:
And scarcely had he Maggie rallied,
When out the hellish legion sallied.

As bees bizz out wi angry fyke,
When plundering herds assail their byke;

As open pussie's mortal foes,
When, pop! she starts before their nose;
As eager runs the market-crowd,
When 'Catch the thief' resounds aloud:
So Maggie runs, the witches follow,
Wi monie an eldritch skriech and hollow.

    Ah, Tam! Ah, Tam! thou'll get thy fairin!
In hell they'll roast thee like a herrin!
In vain thy Kate awaits thy comin!
Kate soon will be a woeful woman!
Now, do thy speedy utmost, Meg,
And win the key-stane of the brig;
There, at them thou thy tail may toss,
A running stream they dare na cross!
But ere the key-stane she could make,
The fient a tail she had to shake;
For Nannie, far before the rest,
Hard upon noble Maggie prest,
And flew at Tam wi furious ettle;
But little wist she Maggie's mettle!
Ae spring brought off her master hale,
But left behind her ain grey tail:
The carlin claught her by the rump,
An left poor Maggie scarce a stump.

    Now, wha this tale o' truth shall read,
Ilk man, and mother's son, take heed:
Whene'er to drink you are inclin'd,
Or cutty sarks run in your mind,
Think! ye may buy the joys o'er dear:
Remember Tam O' Shanter's mare.

WORD LIST

aboon	=	above
ae	=	one
airns	=	irons
bear	=	barley
beldams	=	old women, hags
birks	=	birches
blellum	=	a babbler
boddle	=	a Scottish copper coin
brawlie	=	a well
brent	=	brand
byke	=	a hive
cantraip sleight	=	a magic device
carlin	=	an old woman, hag
chapman billies	=	pedlars
claught	=	clawed
cleekit	=	took hold of
coft	=	bought, purchased
coost her duddies *to the wark*	=	stripped off her clothes
core	=	crew, company
cotillion	=	a lively dance
cour	=	to curb
creeshie flannen	=	greasy flannel cloth
crummock	=	a cudgel
Deil	=	the Devil
dirl	=	to ring
drouthy neebors	=	thirsty neighbours
dub	=	puddle

eldritch skriech	=	strange or unearthly screech
ettle	=	aim, intention
fairin	=	just deserts
fou	=	drunk
fu fain	=	most fondly
fyke	=	fret
gab	=	mouth
gars me greet	=	makes me weep
gart them skirl	=	made them squeal
hale	=	whole
hotch'd	=	jerked
houlet	=	owl
hurdies	=	bottom, rear
ilka bore	=	every chink or opening
ilka melder	=	every corn-grinding
linket	=	danced
maun	=	must
meikle	=	big
mettle	=	spirit, courage
mirk	=	darkness
naig	=	a small horse or pony
nappy	=	ale
noddle	=	brain
Paisley harn	=	coarse cloth
presses	=	cupboards
pussie	=	a hare
queans	=	girls, young women
rair	=	to roar
rape	=	a rope
rigwoodie	=	withered, shrivelled

sark; cutty-sark	=	shirt or chemise; short shirt
seventeen hunder linen	=	fine linen of a 1700 thread gauge
siller	=	money
skellum	=	a good-for-nothing, a rogue
skelpit	=	spanked
smoor'd	=	smothered
swat and reekit	=	sweated and steamed
syne	=	then
tint	=	lost
tippenny	=	twopenny beer, weak ale
tousie tyke	=	a shaggy dog
unco	=	wondrous
usquabae	=	whisky
vauntie	=	proud-looking
wawlie	=	choice
winnock-bunker	=	a window-seat

QUESTIONS

- Are there any other words that you didn't understand in this poem? If so, ask someone what they mean. Try to use some of these words in a sentence.
- In the poem, Tam has a friend called Souter Johnie. Do you know what a 'souter' is?
- Look at a detailed map of Scotland. Can you find any waterfalls called 'Grey Mare's Tail'?

THINGS TO DO

- Why don't you make a model of haunted Alloway Kirk and Tam on his horse, Maggie, being chased by the witches?
- Or you could draw the scene – the kirk-yard and the burn with the running water the witches cannot cross. You could draw Maggie losing her tail to the witches.
- Or, if you are part of a large class, each member could pick a character from the poem, draw it, colour it, cut it out and stick it on to a background like the one suggested above, to make a frieze for your classroom wall.
- Or why not dress up? One of you could be Tam, two people could be the horse, others could be the witches and warlocks. Remember, you will need to make a tail that can be pulled off quite easily.
- Many people in Scotland wore a blue bonnet long ago. It looked rather like a large beret. Why don't you make a Tam O' Shanter bonnet?
- Make a concertina book of a small part of the poem 'Tam O' Shanter'. Each page could show one line of the poem, plus a picture of the action.
- Sometimes, instead of learning the whole poem by heart, people form a group or team of four or five to read the poem bit by bit. The first person reads a section, then hands it over to the second person, and so on. You could try that.
- As you grow older, you might like to learn the whole of this poem off by heart.

May Liberty
meet wi' success

m scenes like these, old Sco
lov'd at home, rever'd ab
breath of kings, 'An hones
ad some Power the giftie

Robert Burns Quotations

grandeur springs, That m

Princes and lords are but

's the noblest work of God

To see oursels as ithers se

The poem 'Tam O' Shanter' is a great favourite and has been translated into many languages. However, it is not the only Burns poem or song to have become famous the world over. Over the years people have used a few lines of Robert's poetry here, and a verse or two there, until these lines and verses (known as quotations) have become very familiar to us.

Over the next few pages are some of the best-known quotations from the work of Robert Burns. Do you recognise any of them? You could discuss them with other people perhaps. Or why not make a book – in class or by yourself – of some of your own favourite quotations and find out what they mean?

From 'Tam O' Shanter'

> But pleasures are like poppies spread:
> You seize the flow'r, its bloom is shed;
> Or like the snow falls in the river,
> A moment white – then melts for ever;
> Or like the borealis race,
> That flit ere you can point their place;
> Or like the rainbow's lovely form
> Evanishing amid the storm.

○ Do you like this part of the poem? It is in English, rather than in the Scots language. Does that sound better to you or not?

○ Do you know what the 'borealis race' is?

○ What kind of pictures do these lines conjure up in your mind?

> 'Nae man can tether time or tide …'

○ What does 'tether' mean? What is the poet saying to us here?

From 'A Man's a Man for a' That'

> The rank is but the guinea's stamp,
> The man's the gowd for a' that.

- ○ What do you think Robert Burns is saying here?
- ○ Do you know what a 'guinea' is? Why should it have a stamp on it? What is meant by a 'stamp' in this poem?
- ○ What does 'gowd' mean?

> Then let us pray that come it may
> (As come it will for a' that),
> That Sense and Worth o'er a' the earth,
> Shall bear the gree* an a' that.
> For a' that, an a' that,
> It's comin yet for a' that,
> That man to man, the world, o'er
> Shall brithers be for a' that

bear the gree = take first place

- ○ Do you like this poem? Why do you think it would be a good thing if the poet's wish could come true?

From 'Man Was Made to Mourn – A Dirge'

> Man's inhumanity to man
> Makes countless thousands mourn!

- Do you know what a 'dirge' is?
- What does 'man's inhumanity' mean?
- What sort of things would make you sad?
  What sort of things do you think would make other people sad?

> O Death! the poor man's dearest friend,
> The kindest and the best!

- This is a very hard quotation for young people to understand because people are usually a bit afraid of death. How can death be a 'friend'? How can death be 'kind'? What do you think?

○ ○ ○

From 'To a Mouse'

> The best-laid schemes o' mice an men
> Gang aft agley,
> An lea'e us nought but grief an pain,
> For promis'd joy!

- Do you think this is a true saying? Or is the poet being too sad?

From 'Address to the Unco Guid'

> Then gently scan your brother man,
> Still gentler sister woman;
> Tho they may gang a kennin* wrang,
> To step aside is human ...

*_kennin_ = a little bit

○   What do you think Robert Burns means in the quotation above?

○   Find out what 'Unco Guid' means.

○   ○   ○

From 'To a Louse'

> O wad some Power the giftie gie us
> To see oursels as ithers see us!
> It wad frae monie a blunder free us,
> An foolish notion:
> What airs in dress an gait wad lea'e us,
> An ev'n devotion!

○   What do you think Robert Burns is saying here?
Do you think he's right?

○   Do you know what a 'louse' is?

From 'Epistle to Davie, a Brother Poet'

> The heart ay's the part ay
>> That makes us right or wrang.

- What does 'ay' mean here?
- Do you think the poet is right?

○ ○ ○

From 'The Cotter's Saturday Night'

> From scenes like these, old Scotia's grandeur springs,
>> That makes her lov'd at home, rever'd abroad:
> Princes and lords are but the breath of kings,
>> 'An honest man's the noblest work of God' …

- The scene described in this poem is of a poor family saying their prayers and reading the Bible together in their house. Do you think that reading the Bible at home should still be an important part of family life?
- What is 'old Scotia? What does 'grandeur' mean?
- Do you think an honest man is more important than a prince or a lord?

From 'Green Grow the Rashes, O'

Auld Nature swears, the lovely dears
Her noblest work she classes, O:
Her prentice han' she try'd on man,
An then she made the lasses, O.

- What do you think the word 'rashes' means in this title? What does 'prentice' mean? (Hint – it sounds very like a word most of you will know already.)
- Robert Burns is making both a joke and a serious point here. What do you think they are?
- There are some very good points here for anyone preparing a reply to the toast 'The Lassies!' during a Burns Supper (see pages 78–79). What do you think they are?

o o o

From 'A Dream'

But facts are chiels that winna ding,
An downa be disputed …

- What do you think 'winna ding' means?
  What does 'downa' mean?
- We have a modern way of saying this quotation – 'facts are facts'. Do you think Robert's way of saying it sounds better?

LOVE POEMS

Robert Burns wrote lots of poems and songs about love. What do you think about the following three quotations from them?

♥ ♥ ♥

From 'Ae Fond Kiss' (Farewell to Nancy)

Ae fond kiss, and then we sever;
Ae fareweel, and then forever!

○ Do you think the people in this song are happy or sad?
Why do you think that?
○ 'Ae' means 'one' – why do you think there was only one kiss?
○ What does 'sever' mean?

♥ ♥ ♥

From 'John Anderson, My Jo'

John Anderson my jo,* John,
We clamb the hill thegither,
And monie a cantie day, John,
We've had wi ane anither;
Now we maun totter down, John,
And hand in hand we'll go,
And sleep thegither at the foot,
John Anderson, my jo!

*jo = dear or darling

- What does 'cantie' mean?
- What does Robert Burns mean by the characters of this poem and song climbing a hill together?
  Why are they 'tottering' downhill?
- Do you think this poem is about old people or young people?
- Have the couple known one another for a long time?

♥ ♥ ♥

From 'A Red, Red Rose'

O, my luve's like a red, red rose,
    That's newly sprung in June.
O, my luve's like the melodie,
    That's sweetly play'd in tune.

- Do you like this verse, or do you think it's a bit sentimental?
- What does 'newly' mean?
  What is a 'melodie'?
  What does 'sweetly' mean in this poem?
- Do you know what a June rose looks like? Does it smell nice?
- Do you think the girl in the poem – Robert Burns' 'luve' – would be pleased to be compared to a rose?

Robert based 'A Red, Red Rose' on an old ballad – a slow and tender song with simple words. Songs like this were often very popular. The tune would have been written by another person, but Burns heard it and liked it, so wrote words to fit the music. It appears that he did this quite a lot.

air fa' your honest, sonsie
Aboon them a' ye tak your
ye worthy o' a grace As la
e ye fill, Your hurdies like

A DIY Burns Supper

When he was a young man, Robert Burns and his friends used to meet in one another's houses, or in public houses, inns or taverns in the area where they stayed. There they enjoyed talking and arguing and singing songs.

One particular house they met in was at Tarbolton, Ayrshire. This seventeenth-century thatched house can still be seen today and is in the care of the National Trust for Scotland, a charity that looks after many castles and other historic sites in the country. Robert Burns and his friends formed a debating club there in 1780.

Imagine the scene. The air is smoky with clay-pipe tobacco, the sound of quarrelling and singing fills the small room. The men sup their drinks and eat hungrily after a busy day in the fields.

What might they be eating? Well, sometimes they ate a haggis. In Robert Burns' time a haggis was a real treat. It was a special kind of food – a 'delicacy'. Nowadays we still eat haggis. Do you know what it is made of? (See page 60.)

Robert and his friends formed a club, but only men and boys could join. This was common enough in Burns' day, though today lots of people think that men-only organisations are wrong.

Because Burns and his friends were not married they called their club the Tarbolton Bachelors' Club.

Not long after Robert Burns died, people wanted to honour his memory. But how would they do this? Someone came up with a good idea – they could hold a dinner or supper in the same way as Burns and his friends did in their Bachelors' Club.

What form would this dinner or supper take?

Well, they could read Robert's poems and sing his songs.

And perhaps they could drink a toast to his memory. After all, grown-ups do that on special occasions. They take a glass of wine or whisky or lemonade or water, or any other drink, in one hand and think hard about the special person or occasion. Then they raise their glass up in front of them and say special words to fit the occasion. This is called a toast, which has nothing to do with bread!

These words are like a salute. They are like awarding a prize to someone special.

Once the special words have been said, the person drinks from his or her glass.

After Burns died, his friends would raise their glasses and say 'Robert Burns'. Then they would take a drink. In this way they were honouring his memory.

Suppers commemorating Robert Burns gradually became more widespread. As the years passed, more and more people who liked his poems and songs would hold special suppers in his honour. Most of these were held on or close to the day on which Robert was born – 25 January.

At these suppers, people also ate haggis – partly because it was a special treat in Robert's day and partly because he wrote a great poem about it (see pages 64–65). It wasn't a serious poem. It was supposed to make people chuckle and laugh. And it still does that today.

We have already said that millions of people all over the world liked Robert's poems and songs, which were written down for people to read in their own languages. They too began to hold more and more Burns Suppers until thousands of suppers came to be held each year, mostly around 25 January – although one or two are held in February, and some even during the summer.

There have been many famous writers in Scotland, such as Sir Walter Scott, Robert Louis Stevenson and John Buchan.

There have been many famous writers in England, such as William Shakespeare, John Milton and William Wordsworth.

There have been many famous writers in other countries, such as Victor Hugo in France, Mark Twain in America, Leo Tolstoy in Russia, and lots, lots more.

Some of these writers are also remembered and honoured at special dinners or other events when an anniversary of their death or birthday comes round, often every 25 or 50 years.

But they don't have a special event every year in lots of countries.

Only Robert Burns has that.

So, you see, he is a very special man.

It is a nice thought that every year all over the world and at around the same time, people hold a party just to honour Robert Burns, his poems and songs.

So here is an idea – why don't you organise a Burns Supper at home, or in your class at school?

It's great fun and it's not hard. The next few pages explain what should happen.

A BURNS SUPPER
PLANNING THE EVENT

Burns Suppers should be lots of fun, but everything must be
planned with care. Start planning well in advance because you will
need to work out the following details.

- First of all, set a date. It is best to hold your supper or party in
  January or February.
- Decide where the supper is going to be held.
- Draw up a guest list, design an invitation and send the
  invitations out to your guests.
- Plan a programme of events – the poems and songs you will be
  using and in what order they will come in the programme.
  There are funny bits and serious bits in a Burns Supper. Try to
  get a good balance.
- Organise some music to go with the event.
- Plan a menu of the food and drink you want to eat at your
  supper. If possible, it is nice to eat traditional Scottish food at
  a Burns Supper. And why not have a glass of Irn-Bru® with your
  meal, or lemonade, or even water? Ask someone, perhaps a
  teacher or parent, to give you some advice.
- Choose someone to be the 'chairperson'. He or she will be the
  'boss'! It is up to that person to welcome the guests to the
  supper and to announce the songs and poems when each point
  in the programme is reached.
- Choose a main speaker to talk about how wonderful a poet
  Robert Burns was. This is for the part of the programme called
  'The Immortal Memory' (see pages 67–68). Pick other people to
  recite the poems you have chosen for your programme.

Here is a suggested order of events for your programme. This is the way a lot of people organise their Burns Suppers.

The Grace

- First of all, the chairperson should welcome the guests with a short speech. Keep it simple.
- Then 'Grace' is said. This is a little prayer spoken before eating a meal. Most people said Grace in Robert Burns' time before starting their food, and some people still do so today.

The Grace used at Burns Suppers is often called the 'Selkirk Grace'. The original version of this Grace may not have been written by Robert Burns himself, but he would have known the original well. It is written that Robert once used an English version of the Grace at the Earl of Selkirk's home at St Mary's Isle, Kirkcudbright, in south-west Scotland. That is why it is known as the 'Selkirk Grace'. Here, however, is the version used at a lot of Burns Suppers:

> Some hae meat* and canna eat,
> And some wad eat that want it:
> But we hae meat and we can eat,
> And sae the Lord be thanket.

*meat = food

- Try to learn the Grace off by heart, but you can read it from a card if that is easier for you.

The Haggis

○ After the Grace, a haggis is carried in to your supper, as if it were part of a formal procession.

You will need to buy a haggis from your butcher or at the meat counter in a supermarket well in advance, and get it cooked or heated up. You can even cook a haggis in a microwave, if you have one. *(Remember to ask an adult before you try to cook your haggis, to avoid any accidents.)*

It might not be easy to find somewhere to cook a haggis in your school. If so, choose something else for your meal.

The haggis is really meant as a symbol. It is a reminder to us of the life of Robert Burns and the type of food he would have eaten over two centuries ago. So it is best to have a haggis, a real one, and one that is properly cooked.

What is a haggis?

A haggis can look like a kind of sausage, but it is usually more like a ball in shape. It is made of ingredients that include oatmeal, beef suet, meat, onions, salt, pepper, cayenne (a spice) and marjoram (a herb). All these ingredients are minced or ground into very small pieces and mixed together.

Then the minced ingredients are sewn into the stomach bag of a sheep. Don't say *yuck!* You don't have to eat the bag!

When properly cooked, haggis tastes delicious. People often eat mashed turnip and potatoes with it.

Where did the word 'haggis' come from?

Some people say that 'haggis' comes from a French word *hachis*, which means 'minced meat'. (The countries of Scotland and France were close allies long ago and would have shared some of their words, fashions and foods.)

But that meaning is unlikely. Instead, the word 'haggis' probably comes from the Scots word 'hag', which means 'to chop' or 'to hack'.

⚬ ⚬ ⚬

Robert Burns and his friends liked eating haggis at their parties. So do we! It's fun, but it has a serious purpose too. What is that purpose? Well, it reminds us of the life and times of Robert Burns and how this famous poet lived.

The Procession

After your chairperson has welcomed the guests, and before the meal is eaten, you need to have a procession to bring in the haggis. This is how to do it.

- ⚬ After the Grace, the chairperson asks everyone to stand.
- ⚬ Now the procession comes in. It includes one person who carries a tray or plate on which the haggis is placed.

Remember, a sharp knife is needed to cut the haggis open during the Address. Please be very careful with the knife – it might be best to let your teacher or parents handle it. Just make sure it is ready for use at the main table.

- You also need to have music to accompany the procession of people when they walk into the supper room.
- The procession normally makes its way from the kitchen, where the haggis has been cooked or prepared. Or, if that is not possible, they can wait outside the door until the right time. At grown-up Burns Suppers there is usually a piper who 'pipes in' the haggis. But you could have a fiddle or a mouth organ to play your music, or a group of you can sing or hum a march tune, or you could download suitable music and play that.

Order of the procession

- The musicians or singers lead the procession.
- Behind them comes the person carrying the plate or tray with the haggis.
- Behind the tray-carrier walks another person who has been chosen to read out the Robert Burns' poem called 'Address to a Haggis'.
- Sometimes there is another person in the procession – a character called Poosie Nancy. But who is she?

When Robert stayed in the village of Mauchline, Ayrshire, one particular tavern or pub he visited was owned by a woman called Mrs Gibson or Poosie Nancy. (The tavern is still there and is still called Poosie Nancy's.) Robert Burns loved going to that tavern.

But what about Poosie Nancy herself? Well, the name 'Poosie' may have come from an old Scots word 'pouss', meaning 'to urge on'. Nancy was that kind of person – lively and fun-loving. She wanted people to have a good time. She welcomed them. She liked to see them happy and enjoying themselves.

In your Burns Supper procession you can have someone dressed as Poosie Nancy as a sign that you are likely to have a good time too. Whoever is playing Poosie Nancy should wear an old-fashioned outfit, that includes a large apron and a white cotton mob-cap of the kind worn long ago. It is a bit like a large white handkerchief gathered loosely around the crown of the head. (Imagine a shower cap with a wide frilly edge.)

Entrance of the procession

So, in comes the procession, with the audience clapping in time to the music.

- The procession stops in front of the chairperson. Then the person who is to recite (say) the 'Address to a Haggis' – that's the proper name for this part of the programme – starts to speak.
- At the third verse of the poem, that same person picks up the knife – or is handed it – and, with a flourish, cuts the haggis open from end to end. (Or you can wait until the poem is finished and cut it then, if you like.) You will find the poem on the next page.
- Then there is a toast – 'The Haggis'! Look for the drink in front of you and raise the glass up. When the chairperson says, 'Ladies and Gentlemen – The Haggis!' the guests answer, 'The Haggis!' Then everyone takes a sip from their own glass.

The procession then marches out again. You should give the person who recited the 'Address to a Haggis' a great clap or cheer as the procession marches out.

You can now settle down for your supper. That, of course, includes eating the haggis on the plate in front of you, which is cooked at the same time as the procession haggis and is made up of the same ingredients.

Address to a Haggis

Fair fa' your honest, sonsie face,
Great chieftain o' the puddin'-race!
Aboon them a' ye tak your place,
    Painch, tripe, or thairm:
Weel are ye worthy o' a grace
    As lang's my arm.

The groaning trencher there ye fill,
Your hurdies like a distant hill,
Your pin wad help to mend a mill
    In time o' need,
While thro your pores the dews distil
    Like amber bead.

His knife see Rustic-labour dight,
An cut you up wi ready slight,
Trenching your gushing entrails bright,
    Like onie ditch;
And then, O what a glorious sight,
    Warm-reekin, rich!

Then, horn for horn, they stretch an strive:
Deil tak the hindmost, on they drive,
Till a' their weel-swall'd kytes belyve
    Are bent like drums;
Then auld guidman, maist like to rive,
    'Bethankit' hums.

Is there that owre his French *ragout,*
Or *olio* that wad staw a sow,
Or *fricassee* wad mak her spew
    Wi perfect sconner,
Looks down wi sneering scornfu view
    On sic a dinner?

Poor devil! See him owre his trash,
As feckless as a wither'd rash,
His spindle shank a guide whip-lash,
    His nieve a nit;
Thro bloody flood or field to dash,
    O how unfit!

But mark the Rustic, haggis-fed,
The trembling earth resounds his tread,
Clap in his walie nieve a blade,
    He'll make it whissle;
An legs an arms, an heads will sned,
    Like taps o' thrissle.

Ye Pow'rs, wha mak mankind your care,
And dish them out their bill o' fare,
Auld Scotland wants nae skinking ware
    That jaups in luggies;
But, if ye wish her gratefu prayer,
    Gie her a Haggis!

WORD LIST

aboon	=	above
believe	=	by and by or soon
dight	=	to wipe
hurdies	=	bottom, rear
jaups	=	splashes
kytes	=	bellies
luggies	=	milk dish for porridge
nieve	=	a fist
nit	=	a nut
sconner	=	dislike, loathing
skinking	=	watery
sned	=	to cut off or trim
sonsie	=	pleasant, cheerful
staw	=	to sicken
thairm	=	gut or intestine
thrissle	=	a thistle
trencher	=	a plate or platter
walie	=	large

After the meal

- When people have eaten their fill, you should entertain your guests with a Burns song. What about 'Killiecrankie' (see pages 73– 74)? Try to get everyone to sing along.
- Now someone should recite or read a short Burns poem, such as 'To a Mouse' (see pages 16–17) or 'To a Mountain Daisy'.

The Immortal Memory

Then comes the most important part of your Burns Supper – 'The Immortal Memory'. What is this?

- Every Burns Supper should have a main speaker. He or she gives a little talk about how wonderful a poet Robert Burns was, praising his poems and songs. Or sometimes the speaker takes just one part of Robert's life and talks about that.

    At grown-up Burns Suppers, the speaker can talk for minutes, sometimes up to an hour! So you can make your talk as long or as short as you like. Five minutes is probably fine.

    But remember, you must call this part of the programme 'The Immortal Memory'. 'Immortal' means 'living forever' and 'never to be forgotten'. Why do you think people say that Robert Burns' memory – that is, the way we remember him – is 'immortal'?

- To deliver this tribute you should choose the boy or girl who will do it best. Listen to him or her in silence. It is nice to show good manners at a Burns Supper.

    The speaker should think very hard about what he or she wants to say. It might be a good idea to discuss the speech with a teacher, parent or friend.

- When the speech is ready, write it down in note form. The speaker may wish to read out the whole speech, but it is perhaps better to learn by heart the main points and to say it without the notes. However, keep the notes handy in case the speaker forgets a point or two.
- At the end of the speech, the speaker should ask the guests to stand up. They should each have a glass in their hand.
- The speaker says, 'Ladies and Gentlemen! Robert Burns – the Immortal Memory!'
- The guests reply, 'Robert Burns! The Immortal Memory!' They should hold their glasses up, sip from them and sit down again.
- Now give the speaker a *big* cheer!

'The Immortal Memory' is indeed the most serious and important part of the Burns Supper. It is a bit like a sermon or a lesson in class. People learn a lot every year about Robert Burns from this part of the programme. Whereas the toast to 'The Haggis' is good fun, the toast to 'The Immortal Memory' is very important.

- At this point in the programme there comes another song and another poem. There can be more than one poem if you have time – there are certainly lots to choose from.

Note that the poem 'Tam O' Shanter' (see pages 27–34) should always be read at some point during a Burns Supper. Most people choose to recite or read it *after* 'The Immortal Memory'.

SONGS

The songs of Robert Burns are loved all over the world. However, not all the songs found in the books of his works were written by him in the beginning. Why was this? Well, sometimes he took old songs and made changes to the original words. Or sometimes he wrote entirely new words for tunes he and his friends liked.

Over the next few pages are two songs. The first is a love song called 'The Banks o' Doon'. The other song, 'Killiecrankie', has a faster tune and you can beat time to it with your hands or feet. It tells about a battle – the Battle of Killiecrankie.

The Banks o' Doon

Play or sing at a moderate pace.

Ye Banks and Braes o' Bonie Doon

Ye banks and braes o' bonie Doon,
    How can ye bloom sae fresh and fair?
How can ye chant, ye little birds,
    And I sae weary fu' o' care!
Thou'll break my heart, thou warbling bird,
    That wantons thro' the flowering thorn!
Thou minds me o' departed joys,
    Departed never to return.

Aft hae I rov'd by bonie Doon
    To see the rose and woodbine twine,
And ilka bird sang o' its luve,
    And fondly sae die I o' mine.
Wi lightsome heart, I pu'd a rose,
    Fu sweet upon its thorny tree!
And my fause luver staw my rose
    But ah! He left the thorn wi me.

WORD LIST

ilka	=	each, every
staw	=	stole
wantons	=	frolics, or moves in a carefree way

QUESTIONS

- 'The Banks o' Doon' is a love song. It has a slow and beautiful tune (see page 70), and is very popular. Although it is a song about joy, it is also about sadness. Why is the singer – the girl – so full of grief? What do you think has happened to her?
- Robert Burns loved the countryside, the green fields and braes, the singing birds, the flowers. But they made the singer sad. Do you find that strange?
- The Doon is a river in Ayrshire. Can you find it on a map of Scotland?

Killiecrankie

Play or sing at a brisk pace.

Killiecrankie

Whare hae ye been sae braw, lad?
    Whare hae ye been sae brankie, O?
Where hae ye been sae braw, lad?
    Cam ye by Killiecrankie, O?

    CHORUS:
    An ye had been where I hae been,
        Ye wad no been sae cantie, O!
    An ye had seen what I hae seen,
        Oh the braes o Killiecrankie, O!

I faught at land, I faught at sea,
    At hame I faught my auntie, O;
But I met the Devil an Dundee,
    On the braes o Killiecrankie, O.

    CHORUS:
    An ye had been where I hae been …

The bauld Pitcur fell in a furr,
    An Clavers gat a clankie, O,
Or I had fed an Athole gled,
    On the braes o Killiecrankie, O

    CHORUS:
    An ye had been where I hae been …

WORD LIST

brankie	=	spruce, finely dressed
braw	=	fine, handsome
cantie	=	lively, cheerful
clankie	=	a knock or blow
furr	=	a deep furrow or ditch
gled	=	a hawk

Killiecrankie – the Background

'Killiecrankie' is a song about a battle that took place on 27 July 1689.

On the one side were the Highlanders, led by John Graham of Claverhouse. He was also known as Viscount Dundee, hence his nickname, 'Bonnie Dundee'.

On the other side were troops mainly from the Lowlands. They were led by General Hugh Mackay of Scourie (pronounced 'scow-ray').

The battle took place at Killiecrankie, in the district called Atholl (Athole = old spelling), in Perthshire.

The two armies were fighting over who should be the King of Scotland at that time. General Mackay wanted William of Orange on the throne, but Graham of Claverhouse favoured King James VII of Scotland (also James II of England) who had fled to France at the time. He went to live at St Germain as a guest of King Louis XIV of France.

The Battle of Killiecrankie was the first battle to be fought by people known as 'Jacobites'. The word 'Jacobite' comes from *Jacobus*, the Latin word for 'James'. Jacobites were followers of King James VII, a Stuart King of Scotland. Like Graham of Claverhouse, Jacobites wanted the House of Stuart back on the throne. The Stuart Kings had ruled Scotland for many centuries until James VII was forced to abandon his rule over Scotland and England, leaving his son-in-law William of Orange to accept the throne in his absence.

At the end of the fighting, Graham of Claverhouse's Jacobite side won the battle, but Graham himself was killed during the fighting.

o   o   o

Robert Burns wrote only the verses of the Killiecrankie song, not the chorus. He tells the story from the viewpoint of one of General Mackay's defeated men. The man states that he survived the battle only because Graham of Claverhouse and another leader, called Haliburton of Pitcur, were killed, thus allowing him to escape.

The words are 'ironic', which means they are not quite what they appear. At first sight it may seem as though the song is sympathetic to the Lowland troops under General Mackay, but in fact the Jacobites are taking the mickey when they sing it. They are crowing over their enemies. They are saying, 'We won! We won!' And they are gloating too by pretending it is one of their enemies who is singing this song, which is based on an old and popular Jacobite song. 'Yes, sing away!' say the Jacobites to this enemy singer, 'but remember that you're a very lucky man to be alive – it is only because our leaders [Haliburton of Pitcur and Graham of Claverhouse] are dead that you have survived – and *we all* know that!'

So what Robert Burns has done here is to take an old and well-known Jacobite song and change it around a bit to make it mean more to its audience. It is very clever.

'Killiecrankie' has a very lively tune. It is called 'An Ye Had Been Whare I Hae Been'. Lots of folk groups sing this song. You might be able to find it on a CD or as a download.

The Lassies

There is one other toast every Burns Supper must have. It is called 'The Lassies!'

- One person (it must be a boy or a man) is chosen before the event to make a short speech about girls and women. It should be a nice speech, in praise of girls and women, but it should be light-hearted too. It is meant to be good fun!

  Have a practice go. Try to think up some jokes or funny things about girls in your class or some women that you know – even your teachers. But be *kind* about it. No nasty jokes. No cruel jokes. No naughty jokes. Just make it good fun.

  Think hard about all the girls in your class. Go on, pull their legs a bit! If you are asked to do the toast to 'The Lassies', ask some friends in class to help you with ideas. And remember, it need not be a long toast.

- When the person chosen to make this speech has finished, he must ask only the boys and men to stand up again. He should raise his glass and make a toast to the girls, saying: 'Gentlemen – The Lassies!'

- The boys and men stand and say: 'The Lassies!'
  Then they take a sip of their drink.

- The guests should then clap this speaker for giving such a funny speech.

The Reply

- Now the girls get their revenge. One girl, chosen before the event, is called upon to give a reply speech. She can get her own back on the boys.

- The girl giving 'The Reply' could ask her friends for help when making up her speech. What do you know about the boys in your class? Try to prepare a funny reply. Make jokes! Pull the boys' legs this time. Make jokes about boys in general. Ask a teacher or your parents to help. They'll know lots of good jokes. You can borrow some of these.

    Your reply need not be long. A few minutes will do. But do try to get your own back.

- This speech is known as 'The Reply to "The Lassies"'. The girl giving this reply should also get lots of applause from the guests when she has finished.

Auld Lang Syne

All Burns Suppers should end with the singing of the song 'Auld Lang Syne'. This song is about remembering old friendships. It is about being happy at having had a good time. The song also means that people hope to meet again and be happy once more.

'Auld Lang Syne' is a famous song and is sung all over the world, especially on New Year's Eve.

Some people pronounce 'syne' as 'zyne', which is wrong. It should be 'syne'.

Nearly everyone today sings 'Auld Lang Syne' in a different way from the song composed by Robert Burns all those centuries ago. It is good to get it right. Over the next few pages is Robert's own version. If it is too long for your Burns Supper, you can leave out some of the verses.

Auld Lang Syne

Play or sing at a steady pace.

Auld Lang Syne

Should auld acquaintance be forgot,
    And never brought to mind?
Should auld acquaintance be forgot,
    And auld lang syne?

    CHORUS:
    For auld lang syne, my jo,
        For auld lang syne,
    We'll tak a cup o kindness yet,
        For auld lang syne!

And surely ye'll be your pint-stowp,
    And surely I'll be mine,
And we'll tak a cup o kindness yet,
    For auld lang syne!

    CHORUS:
    For auld lang syne, my jo …

We twa hae run about the braes,
    And pou'd the gowans fine,
But we've wander'd mony a weary fit,
    Sin auld lang syne.

    CHORUS:
    For auld lang syne, my jo …

We twa hae paidl'd in the burn
    Frae morning sun till dine,
But seas between us braid hae roar'd
    Sin auld lang syne

    CHORUS:
    For auld lang syne, my jo …

And there's a hand my trusty fiere,
    And gie's a hand o thine,
And we'll tak a right guid-willie waught,
    For auld lang syne.

    CHORUS:
    For auld lang syne, my jo …

WORD LIST

auld lang syne	=	old long ago
dine	=	dinner-time
fiere	=	a companion
gowans	=	daisies
guid-willie waught	=	a goodwill drink, a hearty draught
my jo	=	my dear, my darling
pint-stowp	=	a tankard or drinking vessel
pou'd	=	pulled

The Running Order of a Burns Supper

Sometimes people are not sure in what order a Burns Supper should run because grown-up Burns Suppers can differ. Here is a possible programme for you:

1   Chairperson's welcome
2   Entry of the Haggis and the 'Address to the Haggis'
3   Grace and the meal – sometimes the Grace is said *before* the haggis is brought in.
4   A Burns song or poem
5   'The Immortal Memory'
6   A Burns song or poem
7   A reading of 'Tam O' Shanter' – sometimes it is read before 'The Immortal Memory'.
8   The Toast to 'The Lassies'
9   The Reply to 'The Lassies'
10 'Auld Lang Syne'

Some grown-up Burns Suppers have more songs in them. Others have fewer. Some have extra toast-speeches, such as 'To Scotland!', or to the village, town or city where the supper is being held, or to the organisation that is holding the supper.

You might like to have an extra toast – 'To our School!' Indeed, you can make all sorts of changes if you like. The important thing is that you *enjoy* the event. The best Burns Suppers are lots of fun, but good manners are expected and you must remember that the supper has a serious side to it as well – the memory of Robert Burns.

A Shortened Burns Supper

A shorter programme, perhaps for a Burns Supper held during the day in your classroom, might be as follows:

1   Chairperson's welcome
2   The 'Address to the Haggis'
3   Grace and meal
4   A Burns song or poem
5   'The Immortal Memory'
6   A reading of 'Tam O' Shanter', or just parts of it if you don't have a lot of time.
7   The Toast to 'The Lassies'
8   The Reply to 'The Lassies'
9   'Auld Lang Syne'

References

James Barke (editor), *Poems and Songs of Robert Burns,* Fontana, London, 1960

William Scott Douglas (editor), *The Kilmarnock Edition of the Poetical Works of Robert Burns* (verbatim copy), M'Kie & Drennan, Kilmarnock, 1876

Dr James A. Mackay (editor), *The Complete Poetical Works of Robert Burns 1759–1796*, Alloway Publishing, Darvel, Ayrshire, 1993

Mairi Robinson (editor-in-chief), *The Concise Scots Dictionary,* originally published by Aberdeen University Press, 1985

Further reading

Irving Miller (compiler), *Burns for Bairns*, Alloway Publishing, Darvel, Ayrshire, 1990

'A selection of poems or extracts from poems by ROBERT BURNS suitable for reading or recitation by children of all ages, whether in competitions, festivals or simply for their own enjoyment …'

ALSO BY RENNIE McOWAN

The Dumyat Series

Follow the thrilling adventures of Gavin and his friends Michael, Clare and Mot in four exciting books. The first, *Light on Dumyat*, involves robbers, the second, *The White Stag Adventure*, has mysterious incidents at a ruined castle, in the third, *The Day the Mountain Moved*, they go back in time and meet figures from Scottish Celtic mythology, and in the fourth, *Jewels on the Move*, they save some valuable precious stones. Very popular for children aged 7–12, the Dumyat Series is widely used in Scottish schools.

Saint Andrew for Beginners

Read the fascinating story of how Andrew, a simple fisherman from Galilee, became the patron saint of Scotland. *Saint Andrew for Beginners* outlines what is known about the life and times of Andrew, contains a short history of the Celtic Church, and takes a brief look at the other patron saints of the British Isles. The book also includes suggestions for individual and group projects.

Bannockburn for Beginners

Brutal and bloody, the Battle of Bannockburn in June 1314 was perhaps the most decisive victory in the Wars for Scottish Independence, and one that resonates with all Scots to this day. With *Bannockurn for Beginners*, readers can learn about the build-up to the battle, who the key figures were, the tactics, and the aftermath and legacy of that historic encounter.

All titles available from Rowan Tree Publishing, Lochbank House, Castle Douglas DG7 1TH   www.rowantreepublishing.co.uk